31 DAYS
BREAKING NEGATIVITY
CREATING POSITIVITY
AND
MAKING IT A HABIT

A. COLLEEN DONALD

Copyright © 2016 A. Colleen Donald

Editor: Mary Wall

Publishing: Create Space

All quotes and references have been acknowledged by its author and book source. Any original content produced by the author may not be reproduced, stored in retrieval system, or transmitted in any form; electronic, mechanical, photocopying, recording, or any other without a written permission from the publisher and author. Brief quotations in printed reviews and group study is allowed.

All rights reserved.

ISBN: **0692669248**
ISBN-13: **978-0692669242**

DEDICATION

To my mother, my father, and my best friend Keshia McLeod. Thank you for reminding me that I can do anything that I set my mind to and for continuing to encourage me and support me throughout all of my endeavors. I love you all very much!

CONTENTS

Preface

Acknowledgements

Introduction

Part 1	**Taking The First Step**	Pg. 13
	Days 1-7	
Part 2	**Self-Reflection**	Pg. 37
	Days 8-14	
Part 3	**Building Momentum**	Pg. 59
	Days 15-22	
Part 4	**Maintaining Your Pace**	Pg. 83
	Days 23-28	
Part 5	**Complete Adaptation**	Pg. 105
	Days 29-31	

References

About the author

31 DAYS

PREFACE

"Trust Your Crazy Ideas"

It's very easy for people's opinions to discourage your thirst to explore the possibilities of life and for new experiences. I have always had many ideas, crazy ideas (to some) and it wasn't until I was walking through the Target store looking to buy Christmas gifts that I decided to trust mine. It sounds ridiculous, but I found a journal with the words "Trust Your Crazy Ideas" in big, orange print, that sat on top of two pieces of smooth, tan cardboard, with blank pages in between. Seven dollars and ninety nine cents plus tax, and I was ready to write my story. I was ready to jot down all of my ideas and turn them into a reality.

I realized that writing a motivational book was something that I had always wanted to do, but I thought that only internationally known people like Oprah Winfrey, Steve Harvey, and Eric Thomas (people who I truly admire) could do that. Besides, who could I reach, who would listen to what I have to say? I wrote this book for those who are struggling in their everyday lives, who want so badly to succeed, who don't have it all together, but have a dream, have a goal, and are truly in need of motivation to get through their "now experiences." I like to think of "now experiences" as things that are happening now, not in the future, but today. We bog ourselves down so much contemplating the future that we can't even handle what is happening "in the now." *"31 days: Breaking Negativity Creating Positivity and Making It A Habit"* is a simple idea that every day for the next month you will have the encouragement and positive mindset to keep pushing through whatever difficulty that you are encountering. Even on your crappiest days you can relate to the stories in this book and be inspired to conquer your obstacles. I have included quotes, this way, if you don't have the time to read the experience, you will still have a quote to keep you going throughout the day.

Trust that the ideas you have about life, love, happiness, and the things that you want are possible. Trust that you are not the only one that needs support and an extra helping hand; even the people who you admire, your favorite celebrity, a strong family member, or a friend, has been in a tough situation.

I hope that this book motivates you to reignite your passion, and inspires you to live each and every day with a positive outlook!

31 DAYS

ACKNOWLEDGMENTS

This book has been written by from the personal stories of myself and others. I have chosen to change the names in this book to preserve the privacy of those that I have met along my journey. However, I thank those whom have assisted me along my journey and throughout my career

The following people have consistently been supportive and/or have contributed to my growth as an individual. Moreover, they should be acknowledged as a contribution to this book:

Ann Donald (Mother), Darry Donald (Father), Eva Skinner (Grandmother) James Skinner (Grandfather), Myra Donald (Grandmother), Betty Skinner (Aunt), Tonjua and Derrick Williams, Shirley Crumbley, Gregory Hall, Twyla Williams, Patrick Bentley, Thomas (Teijay) Williams, Keshia McCloud, Lawrence Diamond II, Rashad Leaks, Brittney Haughton, and Mr. and Mrs. Ingram.

INTRODUCTION

"Walking in my shoes"

My goal is to share some of my tough times, to help you get though yours. It's not easy being "up-beat" all of the time; it takes work. It's a journey to a positive life style; I occasionally "mess-up" and I occasionally "get down in the dumps." It's not easy keeping yourself motivated; it takes work. I find comfort in watching documentaries and reading books about those whom overcame and became successful regardless of the difficulties they've faced. I am hoping to do the same for you as others have done for me. I'd like to call myself an *inbetweener*. I am successful in my own way. I have made it through storms and I live each day enduring the next lesson, the next season of growth, and I keep going. That's the most important part, to keep going. I have received messages over the years of people confessing to me how much of an inspiration I have been and how much I motivate them.

What they didn't know, (but will, now, after they have read this book) is that I am, too, motivating myself in the process. For 31 days I ask that you walk in my shoes, and help heal and motivate yourself in some of the ways that I did. This is a shared effort. The words on the page mean nothing without application.

This book is for anyone who needs uplifting and motivation. This book is for anyone who is having a difficult time striving towards their purpose. Be open to applying, understanding, connecting, and experiencing something unique. My story and your story are never going to be the same, but we can share our experiences and take notes on how to live out our lives in a more fulfilling and positive light.

PART 1

TAKING THE FIRST STEP

DAY 1

"Everyone has a purpose in life… a unique gift or special talent to give to others." -Deepak Chopra

It's natural for everyone to have that one person who they can tell anything to, that shoulder to lean on when they're feeling down, and that person to call when they have good news. For me, that person would be my mother. But she isn't just that person for me, she is that person for others. Some people define talent as a person who has an artistic ability. My mother used to tell me that she didn't have any talents. My mother couldn't sing, dance, or act, but I knew she was talented. She didn't know this, but she didn't have to do any of those things to be considered talented. There are things that she is good at that she didn't realize. My mother's talents include solving problems, advising, and counseling others. And she's really good at it. She didn't realize it until she found herself involuntarily tangled in her family, friends, and co-workers' personal situations mentoring them through their hardships. Her talents led her to becoming a Cyber Advisor at Saint Petersburg College, where she is aiming to become a Senior Advisor, soon. However, just because you are given certain gifts doesn't mean they are going to flourish on their own. Cultivation is key. Practice is key. Do you think the Michael Jordan's and the Michael Jackson's of the world became legendary overnight?

You have the potential to be legendary and leave your special imprint on the world. You have the ability to make an impact on the people around you. You have to find what it is that makes you special, what makes you powerful, and what your predestined purpose is. This isn't always readily available for us. Sometimes we aren't sure of what our purpose is and we have to figure it out for ourselves. Maybe you aren't a natural artist, but you are a natural at something else. If you take a moment to sit down and think about the small things that you do every day, you will find that you are more talented than you think you are. Harness your strengths and you will eventually find your pathway to succeed in what it is that you were destined to do.

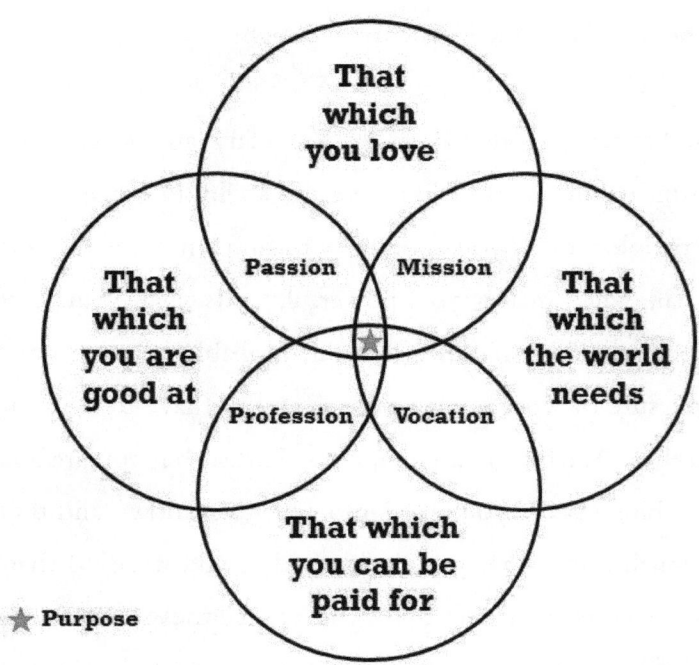

Purpose circles alphabiz.com

Take 10-15 minutes and draw your own purpose circles (use the notes section in the back of this book on page 102). This will help you concentrate your thoughts and get you one step closer to finding your purpose. As stated in the book "<u>Prevail: Discover Your Strength in Hard Places,</u>" "once you find your why (purpose) then the what, the how, and the when take care of themselves."

DAY 2

"Nothing can stop the man with the right mental attitude from achieving his goal; nothing on earth can help the man with the wrong mental attitude." -Thomas Jefferson

I thought that by moving to a new city that everything would get better, that life would get better. I thought that bettering my life solely depended on removing myself from my environment. I was tired of living at home and I wanted to meet new people. At the time, I was drained from everything that I was experiencing in my life. I wanted to run away from all of my problems and start over. It didn't take me long to realize that I had to change my attitude, change my approach, and change my reaction to negative circumstances if I wanted a different result.

"When you change the way you look at things, the things you look at change"
- *Dr. Wayne Dyer*

After spending two years at Saint Petersburg College, I was desperately wanting to leave "the nest" and relocate to a new area. I decided that Miami, Florida was the place to be. It was 4 to 5 hours away from my family which was just enough space for me to have my independence and there are great beaches, of course. I remembered the images that I had seen in movies and I fantasized about the luxurious, big city. I was confident that if I was able to move there, I would have the life that I've always wanted. However, the reality was much different once I arrived. I didn't have any family, friends, or a job. I was having long distant relationship issues, I was struggling with my self-esteem, my commute to class was wearing down on my old car, and my roommates were in every sense of the word, malevolent. The area that I was living in was predominately Hispanic. I wasn't bilingual. This made it hard to find a job and hard to get around. This was not the bliss that I was expecting.

One day, my car broke down at a Pollo Tropical in a deserted area of South Miami. I went inside to ask the workers what the name of the street was so I could call AAA towing services. They responded "Que?" Which I knew, meant "what" in Spanish. They either didn't speak English, or chose not to. (I opted to learn more Spanish after that incident). It was nothing like I'd planned. I had no resources and no idea what I was doing at Florida International University. I knew when I visited the school, prior to attending, that it wasn't the school for me. But I pressed on anyway because I was so eager to start a new life. I allowed negativity to consume me. I cried almost every night and the only time I left my room (extremely small, closet size dorm room) was to workout at the school gym. The gym became my safe house from all of my unhappiness. It was awful and my roommates were the worst of it. I wanted to quit school and I wanted to give up because I was so depressed. I never let anyone from back home know how miserable I was and I rarely asked for help. I didn't try to make things better and I didn't try to meet new people because everything felt wrong. I didn't want to face it, but I wasn't ready for that big of a move. I hadn't healed other wounds that I was dealing with and I hadn't prepared myself for such a big life style change. Nevertheless, there I was throwing myself into a world of new problems. I know that if I hadn't went to Miami with preexisting issues and if I had changed my attitude about my situation, my experience would have been different. I wasn't ready to pursue that opportunity. I wasn't emotionally ready to receive it.

Often we think that running away from our issues will solve all of our problems. Have you ever went headfirst into another relationship, profession, or even a new location without resolving some of your preexisting issues? I'm sure you weren't any happier. If you're facing a difficult issue, no matter how hard or embarrassing it may be, you will have to confront it. If you haven't resolved your issues they will persist no matter where you go, what new job you acquire or what new relationship you form. You have to fix the root of your problems or they will continue to grow. Change your attitude, confront and resolve your negative situations; you don't want to carry that negativity with you and taint other experiences.

DAY 3

"Surround yourself only with people willing to lift you higher"
-Oprah Winfrey

The things that affect people every day are what I like to call, "now experiences." The choices that we make can shape our future and it's important that we realize things when they are happening in the moment. The relationships in our lives affect our attitudes, which then affect our ambition to do things and the availability of opportunities. This isn't a radical concept if you think about all of the relationships you've left, that you've gained, and that you've maintained throughout the years of your life; they have made an impact in some way that has caused you to either remove them or keep them close to you. I've had the pleasure and misfortune of encountering people who've proved to be a blessing and a hard lesson; the people we surround ourselves with can build us up or break us down.

While I was attending the University of South Florida I was dating a music artist. He had little ambition and little will. He graduated a year prior, but met me during his last year of school. Living near campus drained his inability to progress outside of a college lifestyle of partying. After falling on hard times and with the encouragement of his friends, he indulged in immature activities and remained content with where he was in his life. I tried to be his support system when he was down, broke, and discouraged, but his friends had more leverage in his life. They were holding him back by encouraging him to party instead of staying up late and applying for a suitable job. They were encouraging this lack of ambition by telling him that he can always work on his music, but it's more fun to spend money on booze and marijuana. It was tiring for me. He had already graduated college, but was still living the lifestyle of a freshman and didn't acknowledge that he had responsibilities. I never found out what happened to him, but I broke up with him after I graduated college to pursue my dreams; I knew what kind of man I wanted in my life, what I wanted to do, and how much work it was going to take. I didn't want to be held back with him as he had growing to do.

People don't have to be bad people to be a bad influence, or a hindrance to your progress. The choices that you make and who you decide to spend your time with can affect your situation and your opportunities. What are you doing now that is keeping you in your rut, and who is encouraging that rut? Are there people saying to you "that never happens for anyone" or are they saying "you can do whatever you set your mind to?" Are you allowing the people you surround yourself with to hold you back? It is important for you to surround yourself with likeminded individuals; it is valuable to your growth and pertinent to your success.

DAY 4

"Not everyone wants to see you succeed and not everyone wants to see you fail."- Colleen Donald

Networking and building relationships have rarely been difficult for me. I have known for a while that it is something that I need to do to progress professionally. Being a mixed race and a black woman has made it harder for me to grow in areas of my profession. I am not saying this as an excuse, nor am I saying that this is the case for other mixed race women. However, sexism, racism, and colorism does exist in America and all over the world. But that isn't my fault, and I have never allowed the views of others to determine what I want for my future.

I was extremely excited to be hired to work at a radio station. I had only experienced college radio and a television internship up until then, and I felt as though I was headed toward my *big break*. I felt that I was finally on my way to becoming an entertainment professional. I drove to the building to turn in my new hire paperwork. After I turned in all of my documents, one of my supervisors and I walked out of the building to chat underneath the designated smoke break tree. I view smoking as repulsive and a health hazard, but he was one of my new bosses, so I sat in the mist of the polluted air as he asked me questions and proceeded to get to know me better. It was only after a few minutes of conversation that he said "you're the first African American woman that we've ever hired." That made me pause, I was in disbelief.

Within the next couple of days my lead co-worker Christy, told me that our supervisor had recently told her "I like Ashley, and she's not ghetto." He was trying to say that I was a good worker and had a good personality. I know that most people aren't prejudice, they have been bombarded by negative stereotypes in the media that depict certain people or races. Unfortunately, it can cause people to attribute those stereotypes to all people of that particular group. It took me a while to understand that, but now, I am able to educate others and be a positive example. I was able to terminate those original assumptions to most of my co-workers, and that same supervisor ended up being a great friend and mentor to me.

However, not everyone would accept an overly ambitious woman that had only 1 year of paid dues into the company, and who wanted to do more than her position. I wanted to grow within the company, and while working in the Promotions Department was fun, I wanted to learn new skills that would eventually lead me toward an on-air personality position. After much persistence and help from my Promotions Director, I was able to convince the Programming Director to give me a chance as a Board Operator.

This is where my struggle and my blessing became my new opportunity.

Everyone in the Programming Department completely forgot about me when we had a necessary training for a new system. I needed to know how to navigate the new system for my shift that I was working that night. I took grave initiative: I asked multiple times for help and I asked other people who held a similar position to teach me what I had involuntary missed. To no avail. It became clear to me that she (my supervisor) wanted me to fail, she didn't care about my goals, and she didn't care that I wanted to help the company be successful. How was I supposed to do my job if no one was willing to teach me how to do it? I kept looking for assistance because quitting was not an option. There was a man named Corbin who was working for another station in the building. He previously worked with my station before quitting. I would occasionally see him in the hall but never had a conversation with him. I wrote him an email confessing to him my dilemma. Corbin had apparently encountered the same experiences that as I was having. His email response read:

"I would be happy to help you, we have to stick together, it sounds corny but they (this particular supervisor and that particular team) doesn't care about black people here and we have to work twice as hard as anyone else just to get any kind of recognition."

Maybe there are people who don't like you for the way you look, or the things you say, or for just being the way you are. Unfortunately, that is the world we live in, but you can't use that as an excuse or as your reason for you not being able to get where you want to be in your life! Don't submit to those that want to see you fail! Moreover, it could be, that it's not that they want to see you fail, but it's just your dream is never going to be as important as their dream. What you see for your life and the things that you want for your life is not someone else's focus (sorry to burst your bubble). You will never succeed if you allow the way people treat you to stop you from trying to do great things with your life. Redirect your energy to prevailing and working hard to find the right opportunity. There are genuine people willing to help you even if you haven't found them, yet. When you can't find anyone to help you, Google it (that usually works). Your destiny is in your hands!

DAY 5

"Never stop believing in your dreams just because someone else stopped believing in theirs." - Unknown

"You're going to be stuck here, like the rest of us."

I was working at S. Exceptional School as a Teacher's Associate. S. Exceptional School is a school that concentrates on helping students who have behavioral issues and disabilities in succeeding in academia. Most of the students came from troubled, broken homes, or were in foster care, and were below average in all subjects; a majority of the students had juvenile records and were struggling with their social skills. Although I connected with some of the students and I felt extremely empathetic for their situations, this position was not something that I was whole heartedly invested in. This was a second job that I took on to help me reach my goal of moving out of my mother's house and reaching Atlanta, Georgia. I was still aspiring to be an entertainment professional and I knew that Atlanta had great potential. Mrs. Douglas the principal, pensively looked over my resume during my interview and noticed that I received a Bachelor's Degree (you didn't need a degree to be a Paraprofessional in Florida). I knew that I was overqualified for the position, but I applied everywhere else and no one else was hiring at the time. I was desperate. She asked me "off the record" why I wanted the position. I was honest, and I told her about my situation. I told her that I was a recent college graduate and that I needed a job to help me save money. Surprisingly, she hired me and said that she believed in my vision. She was happy to help.

It was time for our lunch break. A few teachers and my friend Patrick Bentley and I gathered around a medium sized table that was positioned in the middle of a room behind our classroom doors. I indulged in small talk. They asked me questions about myself and what made me apply for the position. Once again, I was honest. I told them about my goals and my plans for the future. I told them that this was something to help feed my aspirations for the time being. One of the teachers laughed at me! She'd been there for over 10 years, as most had. She said "you're stuck here like the rest of us." It took me ten seconds to realize that she must have once had dreams beyond the school, but she never had the courage, desire, or will to leave. She was stuck, she was unhappy, and she wanted to push her negativity on me. I responded to her, "no, you're stuck here, I will only be here for a few months, tops." I knew that I replied to her with no empathy, but without hesitation, I shut down that negative statement and broke that negative chain of thinking. I continued my responsibilities in that position for less than three months and I was hired for a better position at Saint Petersburg College.

Speak it, believe it, and you can achieve it! If you allow people to talk you out of your dreams and speak negativity into your life, you will absorb that as truth. Some people have given up on their dreams, goals, or ideas and have become jaded. Don't let that be your truth. Let them know that they can't rain on your parade!

DAY 6

"You have to fight to reach your dream. You have to sacrifice and work hard for it." -Lionel Messi

Take a second to think of something in your life that makes you extremely frustrated.
Math was that for me (yuck).

Saint Petersburg College was a part of my life for a few years. I spent the summer before college there, my first two years of college there, and the year after I graduated from the University of South Florida. I've held two positions on campus, experienced great professors, and great mentors. However, I've also experienced great failures. But those failures became purposeful and necessary to further myself. One of my failures was Algebra.

Although, I could amazingly calculate a sale at H&M, I received my first and only "D" on my college transcript because of Algebra (yuck). I decided that I would try it again because I wasn't going to settle for a (less than) mediocre grade. What I needed to do to change the grade on my transcript was simple, I needed to focus. I needed to focus all of my attention on math. I knew that passing Algebra was what I needed to do to progress further in my education and that it was very important for me to *buckle down.*

I stopped partying, hanging-out as much and I started going to tutoring and YouTube to seek resources that would contribute to completing the course successfully. I gave it my all, even though I didn't like it and I didn't want to. Of course, I would have rather been doing other things, but I had a goal and I knew what I needed to do to accomplish it.

Be honest with yourself. Are you focusing on what you need to do to accomplish your goals? Sacrificing some of my fun-time was beneficial to my future. To be successful, you'll hear it from almost everyone who has climbed their way to the top-you need to be able to sacrifice-just for a while (as long as it takes). I am not saying you can't go out and have a good time, but make sure your priorities are in order and give more focus to what's more important for your future. I will talk about the importance of balance and how learning to say **no** on a different day.

DAY 7

"Those long nights that you often don't include sleep, where you cannot think about anything but succeeding, are the reasons you will be successful."- Colleen Donald

There have been many times that I've wept over my hunger to make a career. There are times where I've felt like I had made a mistake not pursuing a dream more practical. During my first few weeks after moving to ATL, I sat in my bare apartment many nights weeping about how I've put such a burden on myself and my family. How ironic that they were so proud of me for taking a leap of faith and pursing my dreams. I laid in my bed sobbing about how embarrassed I was for not doing more to make them proud. I was poor, struggling to find a full-time job, and relying on them. However, that is one of the things that drives me, the hunger to succeed. When you have no choice, when you have no other option, when you want it bad enough, and you are willing to work for it, it will happen. Even if you aren't in a binding situation, treat your aspirations as if you are.

"When you want to succeed as bad as you want to breathe, then you'll be successful." -Eric Thomas

There is a bio-pic on the success of J.K. Rowling, the author of the Harry Potter series on Netflix. I discovered it in perfect timing; one of my depressed and defeated moods was brewing and her story was able to put things in perspective for me. In short, the movie outlined how she went from being an abused wife and a single mother on welfare to one of the richest women in Britain. It didn't happen overnight, but she never gave up. Rowling loved to write, but for years, she put it off to work at what would be considered practical jobs. Struggling, she finally treated her passion as her last option and she succeeded. She went to many agents, and they went to many publishers. Finally, in just three short years of giving it her full effort and attention, her dreams came to fruition and she became a successful author.

That dream that you have buried deep in your thoughts-you know the one-you gave up on it long ago because you thought it was impossible in your current, "now" circumstances. That is what you need to be working toward. I am sure your dream ended up in your purpose circles from day one. Did you see it there?

Teaching moment...

When I was a child I was involved in many sports and I always liked to try new things. My parents were always very clear on their house rules, but even more so, they were clear about "finishing what you start." I decided to participate in gymnastics one year. However, I decided that I grew fond of other things like music, art, etc. My parents didn't let me quit. I had to go to all of the practices and finish out the year. I had made a commitment and I had to keep it. I wasn't allowed to give up. I decided that I didn't want to continue gymnastics, but I didn't leave my team, or let anyone down that year.

Finish what you start. If you decide that it's not for you, that's okay. But always give it your full effort.

WEEK ONE RECAP

1. Know that you have a gift. Take some time to evaluate the things that you are good at, even the small things.

2. Change your attitude when you're faced with a difficult situation. Instead of being negative think of a positive solution.

3. Surround yourself with positive and likeminded people.

4. Not everyone wants you to fail, there are still genuine people willing to help you.

5. Never stop believing, you've already lost the battle if you stop believing in yourself.

6. You are going to have to make sacrifices to make your dreams a reality.

7. Keep thinking about what you want to do with your life and always keep your eyes on the prize.

ANSWER THIS

What is your purpose?

What are your priorities?

What are some things that you could be putting more of your effort into?

Write down a few positive affirmations.

What can you do to get around some of the barriers in your life?

Do you have certain people in your life that you should consider distancing yourself from or removing from your life?

What issues do you need to resolve or change your attitude about before you can take the next step forward in your life?

PART 2

SELF-REFLECTION

DAY 8

"Start where you are, use what you have, do what you can."- Arthur Ashe

I started two new positions, one in the Promotions Department for the Atlanta Hawks, and the other in the Promotions Department with the Gwinnett Braves. I had never foreseen myself in the field of sports entertainment, but I was enjoying it, so, I decided to "go with it." I was struggling with my finances when I moved to Atlanta, but things seemed to be happening when I needed them. As the basketball season with the Atlanta Hawks started to dwindle, I received confirmation that I would be joining the Gwinnett Braves minor-league baseball team in their Promotions Department. Two part-time jobs was better than none, and I was living near Atlanta, Georgia, and that is where I wanted to be. Moreover, I was available for networking opportunities with many people from all different backgrounds and professions. Being surrounded by people who share the love for sports and have a common interest is the perfect opportunity to start a conversation.

When it really comes down to the wire with your finances, you'll do what needs to be to done to make sure your lights are on. There is no shame in that. The shame comes in when it's something that you know you shouldn't be doing for a greater cash flow. Humble yourself, did you know Grammy Award winning singer/actress Jennifer Hudson once worked at Burger King? That's honest work. I've always held multiple jobs, some not the best, but I have goals to conquer (and bills). I've sold gold and clothes (out of necessity) to jewelers and retail establishments to make an extra buck. I've even used my artistic abilities and sold a couple art projects on eBay. You have to get crafty and take what you have and make it work.

Have you considered that where you are, right now, is preparing you for where you need to be? Would you try to run away from your situation if that were the case? I may have not foreseen myself in sports entertainment but it was God who lead me (purposely) to those positions. I met a man named Montez who was able to introduce me to a lady named Michelle. Michelle owns WSB-TV Channel 182 and she helped me get started with my broadcasting career (one of my goals). If I would have given up working two unforeseen jobs because it wasn't what I wanted to do, who knows if we would have ever met. I know you may be having a hard time with where you are in your career and your finances and don't know where to begin to change that. The best way to begin, is to start where you are, and see where you can find the silver lining that can enable you to pursue greater things.

DAY 9

"Be slow to fall into friendship; but when thou art in, continue firm and constant." – Socrates

In a previous chapter, I wrote about surrounding yourself with uplifting people, but even more importantly, you should have a support system, a permanent uplifting. Having a support system can consist of a small group of close friends, family members, or maybe just one person. Those are the people/person you can talk to about anything, trust them, and count on them to support your dreams. These are the people/person who don't leave your side when things are taking a turn for the worst.

My best friend Keshia McLeod lives in Tallahassee, Florida. She is attending Florida Agricultural and Mechanical University (FAMU) and is a double major in theater and food science; needless to say, but she is very busy. I would speak to her every now and then on the phone when I was having a bad day. Even until this day, every time we speak it's like we never skipped a beat. Yet, after a few months into my move, I started to get glum because I didn't have any friends or anyone to go with to grab lunch and coffee. However, the best things happen when you least expect it. I was blessed to meet an amazing person after living in Atlanta, Georgia for only a few months. She supported my crazy ideas and we had much in common, including the drive to be successful. It was refreshing to have someone on my team, someone there for me while my other friends and my family were away. There were times when I would be emotionally drained, and it was easy for us both to relate to each other, talk about our issues, and find the best ways to resolve them. Friendships can be hard, as you won't always agree with them, their actions or what they have to say. A genuine friend will love you and tell you what you need to hear, when you need to hear it, rather if it's what you want to hear or not. If you have a great friend, a mentor, or even a family member, don't shut those important people out. Don't push your support system away, utilize them. It's hard to be vulnerable when we are feeling defeated, our pride can take over and we can feel embarrassed. However, losing good people over your pride is far more devastating that having a bad day, or having a bad week. Know when you need help and feel comfortable reaching out to your support system. You'd be surprised, good people actually appreciate you trusting to confide in them. If there is someone that you've shut out of your life that you know you should have kept in, call them and apologize. Even if you weren't wrong, you need to keep good people in your life. Step up and be the better person!

DAY 10

"Who, being loved, is poor?" -Oscar Wilde

Love is one of the most deeply sought after non-material things in the world. It's longed after by everyone. Who do you know that doesn't want to feel loved? I know what you are thinking, "I'm not worried about love. I am worried about my life. I am worried about real issues." Bitterness gives us those kinds of thoughts. Without *love* there isn't any *life*. There are many kinds of love and with love is how everything we know has been created.

One of the reasons why we don't have more of what we want is because we don't appreciate what we have. Why would you be given a better house if you can't take care of your current house? Why would you expect other people to love you if you don't show love to other people? We don't love ourselves, we don't appreciate others, and we don't realize that it makes a difference. How can you want more for your life when you can't take the time to appreciate the little things?

I met a man who showed me a lot. He renewed my faith, and helped me, love me. He helped me look at the things that I *do* have, and what I *have* accomplished. I met him and month after I moved to Atlanta, Georgia.

We dated, we laughed, and we loved and had an instant connection. He brought me to church and helped me renew my broken relationship with God. He connected with me like no one else had in a very long time. I hadn't had much, I was stressed, I didn't have a career going, but he loved me anyway. Of course, all relationships have bad moments. I'd be lying if I told you that it is easy adapting to another person's way of being. It's hard at times, but it's worth it. That's what you have to hold on to, "I love this person and it's worth it."

I discovered the book and online test *"The Five Love Languages"* and it really helped me understand how different people operate in a relationship and how differently we receive love. Love is powerful; It will make you feel like you can do things that you have never done before.

However, I've realized that a man/woman that takes you to church, does all of the right things, and helps you change your whole life, is amazing. They can't do all of the work. What if you don't have a significant other in your life at the moment? What if you break-up? What do you do, then? That's why you can't lean on other people or other things for love and happiness. I had to commit to loving myself, bettering myself, and doing better by others. A man or woman, husband or wife, friend or parent, isn't going to do that for you. They can love you and you can still be unhappy. They can love you and you will still be lacking the love you desire. You have to find it in yourself. In other words, you don't need anyone to come into your life and make you feel special, (if it happens, great) but realize you're worth so much more than the validation of others. You are worth more than materials and other unessential things, and in time, those things will come. It's great when you can meet someone that can introduce you to positive things, new perspectives, and a new way of life, but if that person leaves, you'll have to continue your journey without them.

You may have not found your spouse, but you will. Maybe you have, but it is time to appreciate that love, which is something to be thankful for on those days that get tough. Maybe, you have this idea that you are alone. You're wrong. God loves you and will never abandon you. Once you believe that you have that kind of love, it is difficult for it not to guide your life. Start learning to love what you have, love who you are, how to love others, and everything you desire will start looking for you!

DAY 11

"Our joy has to be beyond us, our joy must be greater than our performances."- Dr. Gerald Brooks

You have to learn to rejoice even in your disappointments and your failures. You can't allow the way that people view your performance of something dictate what you are capable of doing. In other words, don't give up on something because you messed up or if you did your best and didn't receive the reaction that you were looking for. You will kill your self-esteem and hurt yourself that way. Depending on the opinions of others is not the best solution to improve. My joy lies in being grateful to be able to make mistakes and work on them. I have joy knowing that I'm blessed to have certain opportunities that other people don't. I am sure we've all had some embarrassing moments. Did you forget a few words in your speech at school? Did you say the wrong thing at work? All of these moments that you have encountered are just that, moments.

Don't let that stop you. Prepare for the next speech, apologize for saying the wrong thing, and maybe make a joke out of it. You cannot find joy in the way you perform, you will judge yourself based on the applause of others. Do your best. You will encounter bad days, you will encounter good days, and on both days you must be grateful and joyful. My mother used to say "take 15 minutes, cry it out, and then get back to work."

Embarrassing moment...

When I was about 18 years old, I was taken to an event in Orlando, Florida by a friend. It was a night festival. There was a reporter who was there to ask the attendees questions about the event. I was chosen and she pulled me to the side. The camera lights were so bright and distracting. She asked me the same question 10 times (seriously 10 times). I couldn't understand her. It was like I could hear but couldn't make out the words. It was so embarrassing. I had frozen. My 15 minutes on live television and I blew it. So I thought.

Who would have thought that years later that I would go on to be a community event host, doing the same exact thing as she had.

DAY 12

"You may encounter many defeats but we must not be defeated."
- Maya Angelou

WSB-TV is a television station under the umbrella of Cox Media Group (a former employer of mine). When I left Florida I thought it would be easy to transfer into Cox Media Group in Atlanta. In Florida, I held two positions at the radio station. Before I moved I made sure I gave them a proper notice with a resignation letter (because the schedule for overnights was made monthly, I gave a months' notice). Most importantly, I was a hard worker. I was confident that I could be recommended to the Atlanta location.

To: Ashley Donald

RE: Letter of Recommendation
September 11, 2014 at 8:59 AM

Hi Ashley! Unfortunately, I was informed that writing letters of recommendation is not permitted. I'm sorry!

From: Donald, Ashley (CMG-Tampa)
Sent: Wednesday, September 10, 2014 11:37 PM

How hopeful was I to think that the same person who wouldn't allow me to get the training that I needed and had been giving me issues on progressing, would give me a recommendation? This was the same station that Corbin (who I mentioned earlier on Day 4) had an issue with.

However, she lied. Below is the recommendation letter from my other supervisor at the radio station.

September 9. 2014

To Whom It May Concern

I have had the pleasure of working with and supervising Ashley Donald for the past two years. Ashley is very enthusiastic and is a very quick and adept learner. She thinks quickly on her feet and has demonstrated the ability to solve problems quickly and efficiently.

If you have any questions, or if I can provide any further insight, please do not hesitate to contact me.

Best, XXXX Director of Marketing & Promotions

This was great news, but it didn't help. I recorded a few names and emails of Cox Media Group-Atlanta employees before I left and I emailed at least 10 employees using my CMG email. I never received a response. A few months later, I decided to do something unconventional and contact one of the news reporters Mark Winne, on Instagram. He responded (the power of social media, is underestimated). Not only did he respond, he offered to meet with me and give me a tour of the television station. I was introduced to various people in the building, including Jocelyn Dorsey who is the Director of Editorials and Public Affairs. A few weeks after that, I had the privilege to job shadow. I met Jocelyn's interns, her team, and really connected with everyone. I was recommended by both Jocelyn and Mark for an Assignment Editor position. I thought that I had an advantage of getting employment with the station. Although, I did very well, I didn't get the position.

There will be many defeats but we must not be defeated. Sometimes, it just doesn't happen when and how you want. It's important to fail, because you are able to learn from your mistakes, improve your skills, and prepare yourself for the next opportunity. Additionally, it can give you the opportunity to create something new. The famous story of Steve Jobs comes to my mind in times of defeat. Below is an excerpt of Jobs' speech to Stanford students mentioned by Alan Deutschman and an online article.

[I didn't see it then, but it turned out that getting fired from Apple was the best thing that could have ever happened to me. The heaviness of being successful was replaced by the lightness of being a beginner again, less sure about everything. It freed me to enter into one of the most creative periods of my life," he said.

"I'm pretty sure none of this would have happened if I hadn't been fired from Apple. It was awful tasting medicine, but I guess the patient needed it.

Sometimes life hits you in the head with a brick. Don't lose faith. I'm convinced the only thing that kept me going was that I loved what I did. You've got to find what you love.]

Don't be defeated, be inspired.

DAY 13

"Faith without works is dead."- James 2:17 Holy Bible

    Do you wake up in the morning with a fresh mindset? If yes, great, that's a start. If not, why? If you don't believe in yourself, and work toward your goals simultaneously, you will never meet them. How can you wake up working toward a goal that you don't actually believe in, or a dream that you feel is out of reach, and expect it to manifest? How can you have faith that something is going to happen from the comfort of your couch while eating last night's pizza, and think that your dream job will fall into your lap? It doesn't make sense. It will never happen that way. I have never seen an interview with a well-established person where they excluded a good work ethic or faith in themselves as steps to acquire success. You cannot skip the hard work and have the faith, just as you cannot skip out on faith but still maintain a good work ethic.

"Faith is complete confidence or trust in a person or thing; or a belief not based on proof." –Unknown

What helps me keep faith in my dreams is something that I learned from Oprah Winfrey. A vision board, is just what it says, a vision, on a board. It can be made however you want, but mostly with pictures of your ideal life and goals. For example: I want to have a nice car, I found a picture of a car that like and I put it on my vision board. Do this, make a visual board of your goals, and wake up every day putting your best effort into making those visions a reality. Maybe you see yourself getting married one day, pick out that wedding dress or tux and put that on your board. It may seem strange at first, but it's a way to constantly remind yourself of what you want. Don't give up! Another thing, write your goals down. Make a plan. Make a tentative list of things to accomplish and state timelines.

My father is the most hardworking person I know. He does anything needed to provide and take care of his family. I greatly admire that about him. I am sure this is where I get my strong will and ideas about preparation. It's important to prepare yourself. He always tells me "you should be preparing yourself for what you want, and when that opportunity comes you will be ready for it." If you want your dream job, but you haven't put in the study time, the work, or acquired the skills to fulfill that position, chances are you are never going to get that job. It doesn't take a lot to purchase a book, print an article at work, or even take a professional class to enhance your skills and make yourself more qualified for your dream job. Maybe you are someone who works over 60 hours a week and you don't have the time. Wrong, there is always time. Joel Olsteen gave a great example in his book *"You Can and You Will."* He said "listen to an audio tape on the way to work, on the way home from work, or while you are on your lunch break." You can even read during your lunch break. Making sacrifices for the bigger picture, having faith in yourself, visualizing your goals, and making an effort to reach them is the way to accomplish them.

DAY 14

"It's important to make goals and visualize them, but it's more essential that we focus on them." – Colleen Donald

While working at Beulah Heights University I became accustomed to our chapel services that were held each Tuesday and Thursday morning. On this particular Tuesday of November 10, 2015, a guest Pastor by the name of Joel Gregory shed some light on goal making.

For the purposes of this book, I'm going to focus on his S.M.A.R.T.G.O.A.L.S: **S**pecific, **M**easurable, **A**chievable, **R**ewarding, **T**imely/**T**angible, **G**odly, **O**btainable, **A**ttitude, **L**ifelong, and **S**atisfying.

The acronym was very enlightening to me and I believe it can help you, too. Let's start with S, which stands for "specific." When making your goals you need to choose a focus. What are you specifically trying to accomplish? If you don't get specific, you won't be able to work on exactly what it is that you need to reach your goal.

Do you want to be a teacher? What kind of teacher? What subject would you teach? What grade would you teach? When would you like to start teaching? Why do you want to teach? Where will you teach? That's being specific with your goals. "Measurable" is the next component of creating your goals. You want to make goals that are measurable, where you can track your progress. If you can't measure your progress, how do you know if you are getting closer or further away from your goals? The next letter is A, this stands for "achievable." This is very important. This doesn't mean what you want for your life has to be realistic, but they do have to be gradually achievable. An example would be owning your own business. Start with a small achievable goals; instead of investing all of your money in a business, make sure you've done your research. Do you have a product? Do you have a logo? Do you have a marketing plan? Start with small achievements that will eventually lead you to your end goal. "R" is for "rewarding" goals, those are the best ones you can make for yourself. At the end of the day, you want to feel good about your decision. Make sure what you decide to put your energy into is something that will give you a rewarding feeling. T is for "tangible and timely." "Tangible is something that you can experience with one of your five senses"- Pastor Joel Green. There is nothing like having the keys of your dream home or the car that you've worked so hard for in your hand. The timely aspect refers to making a calendar for your goals (mentioned in the last chapter). What do you plan to achieve within the next month, the next year or even within the next week? The best way is to write down exactly what you would want to have accomplished in a year, or two, or three! Purchase a notebook and write down how you will accomplish those things. Give yourself daily, weekly, and monthly tasks. Put a deadline on your goals, and don't be late! I will discuss this more on Day 20.

The second half of Pastor Gregory's sermon/lesson was on the acronym G.O.A.L.S. G is for "Godly" goals. I translate this into making impactful goals that are positive and loving. Are your goals something that would help others? Are your goals positive and with good intentions? The next letter O stands for "obtainable," which is similar to tangible and achievable. The next letter is A, and that refers to your "attitude."

Your attitude determines how far you can take yourself with your career, your love life, etc. Having a positive attitude can open doors for you. Making sure your goals are lifelong is also important. You never want to get complacent in achieving, or growing as an individual. Once you meet a goal, make another goal! Lastly, you want to make sure your goals that you want to achieve are satisfying, make sure anything you set your mind to is going to be worth it.

"HE WHO IS NOT COURAGEOUS ENOUGH TO TAKE RISKS WILL ACCOMPLISH NOTHING IN LIFE." –MUHAMMAD ALI

WEEK TWO RECAP

1. Start where you are and do what you can.
2. Build friendships and lean on your support system when things get tough.
3. Know that you are loved. Also, appreciate and love yourself.
4. Don't base your joy on your performances and the opinions of others.
5. You will experience failure, use that as motivation. Don't allow failure to defeat you.
6. Have faith in yourself, but work towards your goals. Faith without works is dead.
7. Create S.M.A.R.T G.O.A.L.S.

ANSWER THIS

What are some great things that you could put on your vision board?

Name one thing you could put more effort into?

What are a few things you thought broke you, but could be taken as a learning lesson (to shape you)?

Find joy(s) in your most recent mistake(s) and record it.

What can you do to be a better you?

What good friendships can you cultivate or regain in your life?

PART 3
BUILDING MOMENTUM

DAY 15

"You are a walking brand and your character helps define you to others."- Colleen Donald

Facebook and social media sites are more than just ways to spend your time of boredom and connect with former grade school buddies. If used correctly, social media is an extremely great networking tool. There was a girl by the name of Brittney that I went to middle school with, I knew of her but I never really knew her personally. That was the only time our paths ever crossed until 2015.

Around the end of March, 2015, I received a Facebook message from Brittney and it read,

"Hey love, sorry I'm late getting you my number. It's funny, a friend mentioned you to me a few weeks ago, said he heard a radio demo or something you did and thought you were amazing! I'm not sure what your goals and aspirations are but maybe we can get together for lunch one day and I can try and introduce you to a few people I know in media/radio if you're interested."

This message was received after she made a comment on my page about how motivational and inspiring I am. We conversed a little, she sent me her number. How strange was it that after 17 years, I meet a girl I went to middle school with and get to know her personally?

She felt a connection with me and wanted to help. We met at Atlantic Station in Downtown, Atlanta. We ate sushi and talked about our testimonies. She entrusted me with two of her contacts and helped me network with more people in Atlanta.

This story is not just about branding, but good character. I touched and inspired someone I barely knew and she wanted to have lunch with me. Posting pictures, statues, etc. can help you or hurt you; that is the power of social media. People are always watching you, even the ones you don't know. Think before you act and speak, you never know who that person knows or who that person will become. Make sure your brand includes a good character.

DAY 16

"Sometimes, you can't ask for advice from other people. Because some people don't believe in living they believe in life, they don't believe in faith they believe in circumstance. You can't allow someone to tell you how to live your life and dismiss faith from your circumstances."
-Colleen Donald

I met a girl named Nicole whose job wanted to move her out of state. At the time, she had a 14 year old daughter to think about. However, she was being offered a promotion and her own office if she decided to stay with the company and relocate. Nicole had a choice, she could relocate to Texas, Tennessee, or stay in Georgia and move about 3 hours south of Atlanta to Savannah. Her first reaction was excitement and joy. The company said that they would pay for her to move and she thought it would be a new beginning for her and her daughter. She drove out to Bowling Green, Kentucky and experienced prejudice and racism. Kentucky was where she would be working, but she thought she could move to Nashville, Tennessee and make the commute to work. Still, she didn't want her daughter growing up in that kind of environment. She received pressure from some of the people in the company.

"It's not that bad, that was just one experience," some said. Essentially trying to convince her to relocate to a place where she knew that she would be unhappy. Nicole thought maybe Savannah would be a better fit for her and her daughter. I went with her to visit the area and Tybee Island. We went and saw the townhome that she decided that she was going to rent and she put a deposit down. It was absolutely gorgeous. Then, we visited Shelly, who would be her boss when she relocated to the area. Shelly lived on Tybee Island, rent free. The company paid for her to live on the island. Shelly urged Nicole to move out to island where she could be near her. We all ate lunch together and Nicole and Shelly discussed the opportunities that were available in the city.

 Nicole and I didn't spend much time there, and on the drive back to Atlanta I could tell that she wasn't completely sure of her decision. She kept asking me "what do you think?" "It was nice, right?" As if I was a deciding factor for her life change. I told her if she was ready for the change, she should go for it. She was being offered a promotion, paid relocation, her own office and she could move into a better home for her and her daughter. However, if she liked her life, she could always find another job and take the severance package that the company was offering her. I told her to go with what she felt in her heart. Her collogues and her other friends told her to take the opportunity. They told her how difficult it was finding jobs in Atlanta, Georgia and how starting all the way over would be difficult. However, Nicole didn't take the job. She didn't feel it in her heart that she should move. Three weeks later she would meet a lady named Rosa with a staffing company that would give her a job making great money and doing something that she loved. Moreover, Tybee Island ended up flooding later that week and destroying a lot of homes. The easy way is not always the best way and some decisions you're going to have to make on your own. Getting advice from your friends and family is great, but you have to do what's best for you and your life.

Speaking of making our own decisions, I have a funny story about my signature curly hair. Everyone loves my hair! I always receive compliments on its fluff and fullness. Most people don't know that I didn't always wear it this way. When I was a kid I would get teased. They would call me "plant head and chia pet." At the tender age of 10 (or somewhere around there) I begged my mom to have it relaxed and made permanently straight. Of course, I was horrible at taking care of it. My mom made sure that I had my hair done every two weeks. However, when I transferred into high school I was on my own (that meant my hair was in a ponytail every day). I finally got a job and decided I could pay for my own hair-dos. After a while, I just didn't want to do it anymore. I hated being under the hairdryer and spending all day at a hair salon. My junior year of high school I decided I wanted have my curls back. My hairdresser at the salon told me not to do it. She said my hair was to pretty to cut. To get my hair back to its natural state I had to cut the majority of it off. I had to start all the way over just like Nicole. But it was a the best decision that I ever made for my hair.

DAY 17

"If you have to compromise your values, your morals, and your integrity, that's not the career for you."- Colleen Donald

When I moved to Atlanta my first objective was finding employment. I left Cox Media-Tampa but I still wanted to connect with Cox Media-Atlanta. That wasn't going so well and I decided to pursue other options. I made a connection with a man named Bain Urke who said that I could help him at the music studio. I had always wanted to be a singer, but I knew that wasn't why I was there. I was there to help promote his current artists and promote his events. I was told that I would be paid for my work and that he would help me with my goals. Bain Urke had over 20 years in the music business. He worked with some of the greatest artists of all time including TLC, Kris- Kross, Xscape, and OutKast. I was sure that I was going to be able to benefit from building a great relationship with him. However, it was short lived.

I knew that it was going to be an issue when he started describing the music industry and the things people have done to make it to the top. He named dropped Rihanna, Alicia Keys, Jennifer Lopez and the like. He said that they all had to give something up to make it. He described the nature of the music industry as one where people performed sexual favors to be as successful as they are. Then he proceeded to question my relationship with my boyfriend. He said that the men in Atlanta aren't faithful and that I should "use what I have to get where I want." He continued, "it's hard to have a real relationship with someone in the music industry because they wouldn't understand the schedule demands." Urke was about 50 years old at the time, he had no kids, and he had never been married because he dedicated his life to the music industry. I told him that I didn't have to compromise my morals to be a part of something and if that was the case that it wasn't something that I should be doing. Also, I believe if you truly love someone you can make anything work.

After that encounter he started to show me more and more why I didn't want to be in his type of industry. He tried to use me for my skills and treat me like a personal driver without paying me. He had me working on inappropriate images for a project which made me feel really uncomfortable. After I refused an impromptu pick up of one his artists from the airport, we professionally parted ways.

As a recent college grad and 20 something, it was difficult trying to balance my polarized view of my current situation. On one side of my mind I believed that I had time to figure out where it was that I was supposed to be. But on the other side of my mind I perceived myself as someone who had fallen behind because I wasn't where other people were in their lives. However, there were a couple of questions that I asked myself when I was making my decision to either leave or continue on that similar path.

If you are contemplating on making a career choice or a lifetime decision, ask yourself these questions.

1. Does it align with my values?
2. Does it align with my morals?
3. Would God be pleased?
4. Do you wake up most days seeing yourself doing it for the rest of your life, or is it more like a hobby that you do every now and then?
5. Would you do it if someone asked you to do it for free?
6. Does it make you happy to do it even when you are in a bad mood?
7. Does it serve a good purpose?
8. Would you be proud of yourself?
9. If no one gave you praise for it, would you still be interested in doing it for a living?
10. Does it help you grow as a person?

11. Are you willing to dedicate an infinite amount of your time and effort into making it a reality?

These are the questions that I created to ask myself when I decided to give up some of the things that were distracting me from having a fulfilling career. I still love music and look forward to having the opportunity to be a part of that industry one day, but it will be on the standards and values that I have set for myself. Every opportunity isn't necessarily the right opportunity. These few questions may not give you a complete resolution to your situation, but it's a start.

DAY 18

"Life is at its best when everything has fallen out of place, and you decide that you're going to fight to get them right, not when everything is going your way and everyone is praising you."
-Thisuri Wanniarachchi

I've been through a lot emotionally in my life. I've been in an emotionally abusive relationship where I felt worthless and unattractive. I've had people that I trusted and that I considered close friends, betray me and make fun of me in my darkest moments. Even as a child I didn't fit into society's ideology of the racial social structure. As Oprah's TV Special *"Light Girls"* revealed, it was hard not only being of mixed ethnicity and having a light skinned complexion but it was hard socially.

"I was too white to be black and I was too black to be white."
- OWN Documentary *Light Girls"*.

It was difficult growing up and having people not believe your real mother was your mother. It was difficult choosing what crowds would accept me and learning which ones deemed me unfit to sit at their table. I had to learn how to adapt in certain environments while maintaining my multicultural identity. It was a difficult time.

Girls would try to burn my hair and want to fight with me just because of what I looked like. I felt alone. I had to experience it alone. I have exceptionally great parents and they are very supportive of me and very loving. But as a kid, I had to deal with things outside of their control. I am fortunate that cyber bullying wasn't as big as it is now, but even that was out of their control. There are many other situations but for the purposes of this book, I'd like to say how those situations affected me in a positive way. I am adaptable, I am mentally able to handle things better, I am self-sufficient, I am stronger and more secure in myself, and I am very outspoken when it comes to gender and racial inequalities. You can look at your life and feel like it is crumbling to the ground or you can use it as a learning lesson and motivator. You can't have anything if you haven't been through anything to obtain it. You can't learn from anything if you haven't experienced anything. I wouldn't be who I am today if I hadn't went through those difficulties.

I read a book called *"#GIRLBOSS"* by Sophia Amoruso who is the founder and executive chairman of Nasty Gal. Sophia recounted her journey in becoming a #GIRLBOSS and of how her life to success wasn't the conventional (A plus B equals C) success story. She had to go through random, stressful situations, and working places she hated to get where she is today. She even wrote about how "shitty jobs saved her life" and how all of those experiences (some unwanted) correlated the perfect drive in her to become the million dollar success that she is today. Those things prepared her for the future.

It's like a message that was sent to me at work; I was having a stressful morning and I received a (very timely) email from one of my co-workers. Rashanda reminded me that the difficulties will happen but you can always come through it with a great victory.

It read,

One thing I've learned is that average people have average problems. Ordinary people have ordinary challenges. But remember, you're not average. You're not ordinary. You are extraordinary. God breathed His life into you. You are exceptional, and exceptional people face exceptional difficulties. But the good news is that we serve an exceptional God! When you have an incredible problem, instead of being discouraged, you should be encouraged knowing that you're an incredible person, and you have an incredible future.

You are destined for greatness and with that comes obstacles. Be excited about the story that you'll be able to share. Be excited that you will be able to teach others how you overcame great obstacles.

DAY 19

"Sometimes it's best to walk away and regroup."
-Colleen Donald

Walking away from people and things that frustrate you can be difficult in the moment. You'll want to react emotionally and say something hurtful. What's best is to walk away and do something else. That's the best way to remain positive in a negative situation. Walk away, think about it, and come back to it. There will always be consequences to your thoughtless words or actions; things that you may regret later. You can use the *walk away* method with anything, it doesn't have to be a conflict. Sometimes, it's best to walk away to clear your mind to alleviate stress.

When I lived in Florida I would go to the beach to getaway and think. When I moved to Georgia I would go to Stone Mountain or to the gym. You may not have a beach, mountain, or a gym, but there is always a way to alleviate stress or to leave a conflict. If you're having a bad day at work take a 5 minute walk around the office. If you're frustrated with a paper for class, go get an ice cream and come back and work on it after you've cleared your head. Arguments work the same way. Tell that person "you're not going to argue" and go into a different room. Delete negative text messages before reading them and talk with that person after you've both calmed yourselves.

Walking away can save you from a lot of pain and stress. My Dad's stress reliever is comedy; he will watch funny movies or funny videos after a hard day at work. Find what helps you relieve stress and use it to combat conflict when it's appropriate. There is no bigger regret then doing something in the heat of the moment without thinking it through. Take a deep breath, walk away, and regroup.

With face to face confrontations, say the exact *opposite* of how you feel. It sounds strange, but try it. For example if you're upset with a friend for being late to an event (like how I normally am). Say to your friend, in a genuine tone, "thank you for taking the time out of your day to be here for me, I appreciate you." Instead of how you may truly feel in the moment. I guarantee that your friend will be the first one to apologize and strike up the conversation about their late arrival. Then, after the event, say something along the lines of "I understand that you may have had things to do, but next time, can you just let me know that you are going to be a little late, just so I can prepare for it? Love you, thanks for coming!" Use your own words but make it genuine and kind. Choosing the right choice of words to express how you feel can be difficult to do when you are upset. That's why, in my example, it would be easier to make the compliment, attend the event, and then express how you feel in the polite way afterward.

My mom always tells me "it's not what you say, it's how you say it." With an email or a text message, (which are horrible ways to communicate feelings) if you must, take 10 minutes and go do something else before you respond to someone that says something that you don't like. This gives you a calm down period before you make a hasty comment. It's important to know that everyone doesn't think, feel, see, or understand things from your perspective. Communication is key to breaking down the barriers, and sometimes walking away and regrouping is the best way to help avoid negative situations.

DAY 20

"Our daily decisions and habits have a huge impact upon both our levels of happiness and success." -Shawn Achor

In the book *"Living Well, Spending Less –12 Secrets of the Good Life"* by Ruth Soukup, she discusses the importance of creating good habits. Creating good habits sounds easier said than done. I know this. It took me a very long time before I was able to drink the recommended 8 glasses of water a day. Ruth explains how "creating good habits are the key to getting things done."

When you make everything that you need to accomplish a part of your daily routine, it will help you achieve even your smallest goals. Organize your day in the same way that I wrote about focusing your goals on Day 14. Make achievement a habitual goal. I have a binder and a planner that I carry with me every day. I write down what I need to do for the day and I check off my list as I go. If I can't complete all of my tasks for that day, I move them over to another day to complete (but only if I put too much to handle on my plate that day). I never want to get in the habit of procrastination, that's not a good habit to have.

What does creating good habits have to do with accomplishing goals, and what does organization have to do with focusing your goals? Everything. Let's start with creating good habits. Suppose one of your goals is to lose weight (isn't everyone's), creating a habit of waking up early to go take a walk before work will help you accomplish that goal (along with eating healthy). Another example, let's say you want to buy a new car. Make it a habit to put aside five dollars for every time you make a purchase and 100 dollars for every time you get paid from work. Depending on how you've organized your goals (your priorities) that will determine how fast you accomplish them. Which brings me to my point of how organizing your goals helps you focus them. As I briefly discussed on Day 14, write them down and put a timeframe on them. Write, "I want to lose 20 pounds in 3 months or I want to buy a new car within the next year." That will help you focus. Make a commitment to yourself. Creating good habits will help you focus on those commitments. It won't seem as tasking and as difficult if it is a habitual goal. Habits are things that we don't have to think about, we just do those things naturally. Essentially, you'll be able to focus on your goals without thinking about them because you've made the steps to accomplish them habitual. Isn't that great?

I read an article in Forbes about a husband and wife who saved 40,000 dollars in two years. They wanted to travel the world. So they sacrificed (Day 6), They created better habits and organized themselves (Day 20) and they supported and leaned on each other in difficult times (Day 9, 13, and 14). They sacrificed by not splurging and they were frugal with their purchases. They knew that they wanted to save a specific amount of money for a certain amount of time. The couple organized themselves by paying off their debts and made sure they knew where to put, and how to use, their money. Lastly, they did it together. They supported each other and conquered their hard and difficult times by encouraging each other and kept each other focused on the prize (Day 9 and 10).
Now, it's your turn. Get started today! Create good habits, organize yourself, and watch your dreams come to fruition.

DAY 21

"Adapt when expectations aren't met, adjust when plans don't follow through, and be open to finding new ways to achieve your results. But most of all, pray."- Colleen Donald

A big part of remaining positive and staying motivated is adjusting to our "now experiences." I make plans all of the time, I organize, I make good habits, I'm kind to others, and I try to do everything possible to make things go my way. The reality is, it won't always go my way (or yours). As I mentioned on Day 13, disappointing things will happen no matter what. Disappointments go beyond our goals. There are disappointments in our relationships, our friendships, and our family. We have to deal with divorce, broken promises, heartbreak, job loss, and financial difficulties.

All of these things weigh heavily on the minds of people like you and I every day. It doesn't stop there. What about when you have to go to work with a horrible boss, your marriage has fallen apart, you're living pay-check to pay-check, and you have kids to worry about? What can you do about that? How can you stay positive when so many other negative things are going wrong and when it seems like one thing after another is falling apart? Well, worrying won't help. Prayer and positive endurance will. After I give it to God I have to know that it will be handled, but I also have to endure it with grace until the situation ceases. As do you. You must adjust, accept the situation, and use your heart to guide you decisions (Day 16).

Trust God. He will lead you and he will help guide you and be with you in times of uncertainty. When you believe in your heart, and pray from your heart, things may not change right away, but they will become easier to handle. I've had my dark days. I've thought about making selfish actions, I've thought that there was no hope for anything better. But guess what? It did get better. Think about the last time, that you thought, it was the last time. Did you not make it through that storm?

If your heart says fight, than fight. Fight for your marriage, your friendships (the right ones), and always, fight for your life. If your heart says leave your job, make plans and find another. We can't get so comfortable in our plans that when they don't go according to how we wrote them that we are so willing to give up or so complacent to stay where we shouldn't be. You'd be surprised how you can create unnecessary "weight on your shoulders." Instead of wallowing in your misfortunes or painful circumstances think about ways to *resolve* them. Put your effort into fixing the situation. How can you *fix* your finances? Are you able to get a second job until you can get back on your feet? Can you sell some of your items that you don't need or use? Can you cancel some credit cards? Can you spend a little less (or a lot) and save more? Think about solutions rather than spend your time thinking about what is happening in the "now." Moreover, the moment won't last forever. So don't get caught up thinking about it. I've never imagined myself going through half of the good or bad things that has happened to me. But that's all a part of the journey.

Usually, when people get fed-up or when they have decided that they have reached their breaking point, that is when the real resolutions are made. That is when we become serious about changing the situations that we don't like or at least, find the best ways to deal with them. I am hoping you don't reach that point. Don't put off tomorrow what you can do today. Start reevaluating your situations and making efforts to resolve them by coming up with solutions. If no solution can be completed at the moment, endure the moment with your head held high until you can resolve the situation.

Again, these are just moments, they will not last forever.

Personal moment...

Break-ups are painful, there is just no way around that. You are never prepared to have your heart broken. I have been heartbroken, many times. There is always that one, that hurts the most. I was looking at houses and making plans with a guy that I thought I was going to marry. He left me, through a text message, stopped talking to me, and ignored me. Of course, there were differences and issues, but it was the way that he did it that hurt the most. Showing no care, as if I was someone who had been there just to pass the time. I went through the motions of being sad and distraught. I asked God to "fix it." He never answered me. I asked God to "fix him." He never answered me. Then the moment came, God was saying "fix your own life." Focusing on yourself and bettering yourself will draw the right people into your life and you won't have to "fix" anything. Sometimes all of the effort we put into others, we should be putting into ourselves.

WEEK THREE RECAP

1. Branding yourself well, having good character, and building connections is pivotal to your success.

2. Be careful when taking other people's advice. Sometimes it's best to stick with your intuition and let your faith and heart guide your decisions.

3. Ask yourself the 11 questions that are on Day 17. Make sure you aren't compromising yourself and who you are for your dreams.

4. You are destined for greatness, and with that comes struggle and strife. Embrace the struggle.

5. Take a break when faced with difficult situations. Walk away and regroup.

6. Create good habits, organize yourself, and watch your dreams come to fruition.

7. Be adaptable and be able to adjust when things don't work out the way you originally planned.

ANSWER THIS

What can you adapt to and what can you change in your life?

Name one thing you could put more effort into?

How can you better handle your stress?

How can you better organize yourself?

What can you do to better your character?

Are compromising your authenticity in some areas of your life?

Are you making decisions based off of the opinions of others?

What good habits are you going to implement into your daily routine?

PART 4
MAINTAINING YOUR PACE

DAY 22

"Patience and perseverance have a magical effect before which difficulties disappear and obstacles vanish." -John Quincy Adams

The hardest thing in my life I've had to deal with is developing patience. I've grown up in the "microwave" era of wanting things fast and wanting things to happen, now. Even though I've read the stories about Steve Harvey and Tyler Perry who were homeless at one point before their success. Even though I've seen the documentaries of how people leave the poorest of countries and go through so many difficulties just to become an American and make a different life for themselves. And even though I know that Steve Jobs (who became one the most successful people in technology development) took years to reach his goals, I still want things to happen for me when I want them to. I've done everything from trying to develop two online shows, record music in a storage unit, create Instagram news story videos, sent emails, made phone calls, gave-out my resume in person, and job shadowed various people in all facets of the broadcasting and entertainment industry. I've worked in radio, I've interned, I've created websites. Why isn't it *my* time yet? Then, I started to question, why is everyone else moving forward and I'm at a standstill? I thought that, at least, if my career isn't going as planned, that I should be happily married and with kids while working toward regaining control over it.

It's a hard thing to stop thinking about (especially if you are a social media junkie where all of your friends display only the best parts of their lives), but I had to learn that *comparison is a dream killer*. Everyone has a journey to get through to get to where their destiny is. Your chapter 12 isn't going to look like someone else's chapter 30. Things take time and they will only happen at the *right time*.

Sometimes we feel like we are doing everything right and it seems like nothing is happening. We have faith, we pray, we take action and nothing is happening. Even though your circumstances may be different than mine, everyone gets a little frustrated when things are not happening as soon as they had imagined (no matter what it is). That's why developing patience is very beneficial for anything that you want to accomplish. Good things happen, but great things take time. When you are doing all that you can, what else can you do?

Your life is like wine. It can take up to a year to have a good bottle of wine, and the most valued wine (and expensive) is usually aged way beyond that time span. Think of yourself as a bottle of wine that is acquiring skills, wisdom from your experiences, and that it is developing a fine, positive spirit. You are a bottle of wine that's not completed and not ready to be offered up to others. Wait until you are aged to promise.

"Everything thing you are going through is preparing you for what you asked for."- Unknown

Patience is needed among all of the other skills that are needed to be positive and successful. Have you ever heard the saying "in due time?" When it's your time, it will happen. That "it" could be something that you never imaged for yourself, something you've always wanted, or that "it" could be the opportunity you thought you'd never ask for. Whatever that "it" is, it will be *just for you* and it will be at the time that it's supposed to happen. Don't compare your process or rush your process, that would ruin the outcome! Don't be the cheap wine that gives people headaches!

DAY 23

"The secret of happiness lies in looking at all the wonders of the world and never forgetting the two drops of oil in the spoon." - Paluo Coelho

After reading "The Alchemist" by Paluo Coelho, I realized how simple, yet powerful, his narrative had affected me. One of the takeaways was that balance is the key to a happy life. His example about being able to keep the oil in the spoon and still be able to realize all the beauty around the world resonated with me. Simply put, be able to balance a life of responsibility and also enjoy yourself. This can be difficult for someone who is very dedicated to their career. For example, according to the National Association of Law Placement, a lawyer works a minimum of 2000 billable hours a year, which doesn't include pro bono work and the actual hours that they put in. After visiting various Law blogs with responses from a variety of lawyers such as AVVO.com, some lawyers work 60-70 hours a week and some even make themselves available 24/7 on an emergency basis. That's a lot of hours.

How can someone who works so many hours, or someone that has so many responsibilities be able to enjoy the wonders of the world? How can someone make the time to enjoy new experiences? With an honest effort, and practicing the word **no**.

For over-achievers, like myself, this took some practice. There should be a balance of adventure and responsibility. Just as there should be family and me-time. Planning will help with this (as mentioned in previous weeks), but making an effort to take action and learning to say **no** to some people, opportunities, and great things may be your best shot at exploring the wonders of the world.

Saying **no** can be difficult if it means missing out on something great. For example, let's imagine that you work at an incredible job (insert your dream job) and you've achieved where you've always wanted to be. However, you don't spend as much time with your family that you would like. But you are able to manage and have a great and happy life. One day, your boss calls you into the office and says that he/she would like to promote you to another position. This is something that you never expected. Even though you have a happy life, it will grant you more money, and a better title at work. Unfortunately, it will cause for you to spend even less time with your family, and more hours at work. This means, the trip to Colorado will be canceled and less family projects to participate in. Of course, this is a hypothetical situation. But a very possible one. Would you say **no**? Would you accept the new title and let the money entice you? Are you able to balance the oil in the spoon *and* be aware of all the great things around you? Balance is the key to a happy life. Life is too short to push papers around and have nothing but material things to show for it. Make memories and keep a good balance between your career and your social life (**no**, it can't be the same thing).

DAY 24

"Health is not valued until sickness comes." - Dr. Thomas Fuller

We all know that food can affect your health, but health is not only to be a concern of the physical body; it is also to be a concern of your mental and emotional health. Some researchers say that food can affect your mood.

"The link between emotions and eating is no myth," Sherry L. Pagto, PHD, associate professor of preventive and behavioral medicine at the University of Massachusetts' Medical School in Worcester. She continued "People do eat to feel better, so the link is there" -everydayhealth.com. Have you ever heard of the saying "you're not you, when you're hungry?" (Snickers commercial) or "after this sugar rush I'll probably crash later?" From my personal experience, it's true. Take heed to your body and what it is telling you. I'm not saying go on some fanatical diet. But when you eat better you feel better. Research what foods could be beneficial to help you. I've done my own personal study. I was dedicated to eating clean and drinking water, green tea and ginger tea. Within the first week, I experienced being calmer and less agitated with things that I would normally get myself worked-up about. Start to cleanse your mind, body and spirit by eating healthier foods.

In the bible, fasting was noted as a process to help align your thinking and body with the spirit of God by purging certain foods and certain desires. In short, not only is it important to focus on the certain types of foods we eat, but it is also important to focus on what we are feeding our soul. This brings me to what I like to call emotional cleansing. The idea is simple, the same way you that need to cleanse your body of toxins to help you think and feel better, you also need to cleanse your mind of negative thoughts (the essence of this book), and cleanse your environment of negative people (as discussed in week one). We can take a step further and expand on the idea of removing other people and negative things from our surroundings by working on changing ourselves. I read a very enlightening book called _"The 40 day Soul Fast- Your Journey to Authentic Living"_ by Cindy Trimm. This book was more focused on cleansing the "self" the internal soul and not your external surroundings. That's something to think about. Growing spiritually and owning up to your responsibilities by implementing new thoughts and ideas. Some characteristics mentioned in her book are similar to the ones I've already shared with you: patience, balance, passion. I believe that healing yourself first is key to becoming a more healthy and vibrant you.

Try this, for 4 weeks stop eating greasy and fried foods. Drink more water, tea (lightly caffeinated) and stop drinking coffee, soda, and sugary drinks. Write down how you feel each day. At the end of it, you may be surprised on how much better you will feel and how much clearer your thoughts are!

DAY 25

"Continue to be you, it matters."-Colleen Donald

It's easy for us to succumb to our negative experiences and lose ourselves in life's transitions and unexpected obstacles. The most detrimental thing we can do is lose the essence of who we are. After all, this discussion about building good relationships and planning the future is stressful. It makes you think about your decisions, and if you are making the right ones. It makes you think about what you really want, and if all of this hard work is worth the fight. It's probably forcing you to examine every single detail about yourself (especially when we are discussing cleansing souls). The problem isn't that you've all of a sudden "lost who you are" it's that you have to continue to remember who you are throughout your process. The good parts of you are still in there!

I honestly never knew that who I was mattered to anyone but my family. It wasn't until I had a long conversation with an old college friend about how he viewed me. I had just gone through a break-up and naturally I was distraught for a few days (okay, completely devastated). I was becoming everything but who I was naturally. I wasn't being productive, I had no energy, and I cried, often. I was eating poorly, shying away from people and just miserable. I had thought it had to be because I am not pretty, I'm not good enough, I'm just not perfect enough for him. That wasn't it at all. Now, it wasn't completely my fault. But after talking with Daryl, he assured me that I too, was to blame. One thing, it was because I stopped being "who I really am." I stopped being the person I was when I met him. In fact, I had stopped being myself to everyone. Before my hard times, I was inspiration, I was confidence, I was support and motivation. When my life started to dwindle in the most negative direction, my personality, my appearance, my attitude, and my health did also. All the little things that encompass who I am, were dismissed and I started to be a "people replant."

I'd like to insert a disclaimer: anyone who left you during your hard times was never meant to have you in your best times. People who truly love will be able to weather a storm or two. You will never be perfect.

Even to the people who do love you, the little things still matter. Your smile, your hug, your encouraging words, your support, and positivity. People notice the changes even when you try to hide them. I would stop posting my Facebook inspirations and encouraging words and I would get messages saying "hey what happened to you."

If you allow the things in your life to discourage and change the great things about you, how can you expect anyone to want to be around you? Should every conversation you have with your friends be about how miserable your life is going, should every conversation with your significant other be about how unhappy you are? Suppressing and controlling emotions are two different things. Learn to not share too much, but still get the support you need. Be someone that people enjoy being around, be strong, be the best version of you. Wake up and ask yourself each day, "will I make today a good day?" In closing, don't let your circumstance compromise the nature of your presence. Your behavior can block your blessings and ruin some of your relationships.

DAY 26

"Change will not come if we wait for some other person or some other time. We are the ones we've been waiting for. We are the change that we seek." -Barack Obama

Make a change. One of the reasons why we find ourselves unhappy is because we aren't doing the things that make us happy. What if you don't know what makes you happy? Not only would this be the best time to do some soul searching, faith renewal, and purging of the things that *don't* make you happy, but this would be the best time to try new things. Why? Because you are *ready* to make changes. Changes are made when you are *completely* uncomfortable in where you are. Changes are ready to be made when you are at your end. With that *end* becomes a new *beginning*.

I spoke with a woman named Cat at an event I was working. Cat is a Mary Kay consultant. Naturally, she wanted me to try Mary Kay products, so, she gave me a call later that week and invited me to her home. I brought my friend Michelle and decided to make it a girls day. While speaking with Cat, she told us her story about being a double graduate and that she is currently an architect. I found that odd. Why would someone who went to college and has a good paying job as an architect want to sell Mary Kay products?

Simple, she wasn't happy. Cat told us that she only worked as an architect for the company 3 times a week. She wasn't interested in being an architect forever and wasn't quite able to work with Mary Kay full-time, even though she loves it. The thought of the day-in and day-out negativity, sitting at a desk all day, and being an architect for 20 years to retirement wasn't what she saw for her life. For her it wasn't worth the money. Her wants had changed. She told us that she would have "never in a million years thought that she would be a consultant with Mary Kay." In fact, she said that she teased her friend who had introduced her to the company for being involved in it. However, completely ready for a change, seeing how it would be beneficial for her, and realizing she may actually enjoy it, she took the risk. She ended up completely loving it. She wants to be a full-time consultant and continue to grow with the company.

Now, maybe you don't need to make a complete career change, but you should definitely pick up a hobby or something that takes you away from the everyday stresses.

Sometimes we have to take risks for our happiness. You are sure to fail if you never try, but you'll never know until you give it a chance. Are you taking risks for your happiness? Is what you are doing now, at this moment, something that you foresee yourself doing for the rest of your life? Do your future plans align with where you are?

"Make a decision to take a chance and make a change."- Unknown

DAY 27

"The weak can never forgive, forgiveness is an attribute of the strong." - Mahatma Gandhi

Forgive yourself, forgive others, and move on. How easily is it to sulk in our failures, disappointments and our could of, would of and should have been? Very easy. The truth is, none of those things happened for you and there is nothing you can do to change the past. All of the crying, the complaining, and the "beating yourself up" won't do anything to change the past. Nothing. Can. Change. Your. Past. So where is your focus? Your focus is on today, then tomorrow, and then your future. Forgive yourself for your *human* mistakes and forgive others for their *human* mistakes. The only way to heal yourself from pain is to forgive.

Forgiveness is for you, not for the other person. If you've never heard this before, I am glad to be the one to free you from the thought that forgiveness is for everyone else. The person that hurt you, lied to you, or stole from you, is not thinking about how mad they are at you for letting them do that, right? No. You are the one that's mad at yourself for allowing them to treat you and do those things to you. So, you are the one who has to forgive, because you are the one who has to live with it. Do you want to live with it? Is it worth every time you see that person for your whole day to be in ruin? I don't think so. Forgive them, forgive yourself and move on. Learn from the experience, and know that person wasn't a good friend, person, or mate for you. Be happy that you were able to realize it, and believe me, they will eventually realize their mistake (and when they do, you will still have to be forgiving). There is a peace in forgiving. Don't let pain hold you hostage and prevent you from moving forward with your destiny.

"Throw it off. Whatever they did and whoever did it, it's not worth it. Don't allow your history to abort your destiny. If you want to be in power you have to be able to shake it off. Too much in front of you to be incarcerated and bound by them, let it go." -T.D. Jakes (Blessed Attitude)

DAY 28

"In about the same degree as you are helpful, you will be happy."
-Karl Reiland

The satisfaction you get from helping others is a feeling like no other. We often walk around self-entitled and selfishly only concerned about our own wellbeing. We become so consumed in our everyday stresses and complaints that we often forget that we aren't the only ones in pain. I have found it to be easy to remain positive in my pain while helping others through their pain. Sometimes, it's not about sharing your pain, it's about helping others get to their healing and that action tends to heal you in the process.

I was covering the Shining Light Recovery Home Winter Gala event for SCB-TV Channel 182. The recovery home's mission is to "help release women from the bondages of drug and alcohol addiction to lead a life in Jesus Christ." The event was to help raise donations and sponsorship for an additional building that would be able to house more women for the 12 step recovery program. While walking around interviewing board members and event attendees, I had the chance to speak to a few of the women who had since graduated the program. These women told stories about losing their families, their homes, and their entire lives because of their addictions. "I was addicted to heroin" one said. "I was thrown in jail and lost everything" another said. I sat in aw; because these women were beautifully made, and their appearance didn't match the nature of their journey. I even spoke to one woman that was grateful because she was able to tell her story out loud and that she didn't think she would be able to do that. I didn't think about myself in these moments. I didn't think about my pain that I was feeling in my life. I felt compassion. I was helping these women, whom have had it (I would say) a lot tougher than me. I thought badly about my life all day complaining about trivial things, things that were happening in my life that were nothing compared to the stories of these warrior women.

There is a saying, "if everyone around us poured out all of their problems on the floor, even the ones that others can't see, and we had to choose, I am sure we'd all want to choose our own problems."

After that event, I decided that one of the best ways to get through my pain was to help others through theirs. I volunteered with Habitat of Humanity and I had a blast using power tools and helping build a home for those in need. It just feels good to know, even in my dark times I can make someone smile.

We have to be more grateful, our circumstances are not the worst (even if we feel that way). None the less, times do get extremely difficult. Help someone else in your time of need. Bless someone else in your time of despair. You'll start to notice how less empty and less heavy you feel by the end.

"WE RISE BY LIFTING OTHERS"
– ROBERT INGERSOLL

WEEK FOUR RECAP

1. The things that you want are not going to happen right away; you'll need to keep patient and push through the process. The path that is yours will be *yours only*.

2. One of the great secrets to happiness is balance. You must be able to work hard but still be able to say **no** to somethings in order for you to enjoy your family and your hobbies.

3. Keep your health (mind, body, spirit) in a virtuous standing.

4. Don't allow your circumstances to change your positive behavior.

5. Change is necessary for growth and happiness, "take a chance to make a change."

6. Forgive. Forgive. Forgive.

7. Help others heal and heal yourself.

ANSWER THIS

What necessary changes should you make for your health (emotional, physical, spiritual)?

What things do you need to say "no" to, to help balance your life?

How will you go about forgiving those who have wronged you?

Who can you help or volunteer for that is in need?

Do you allow negative circumstance to change you behavior?

How can you practice patience in your life?

PART FIVE

COMPLETE ADAPTATION

These are the necessary things to do in order to complete the process.

DAY 29

EVALUATE

It's time for you to sit down and *evaluate* your life. Take a moment to think about your life as it is, and start with what you have. Think about what practices should remain in your "new way of being." The past 28 days have prepared you for this; I have given you examples and good places to start. Set out some time where you can think about all of this information, let it soak in and prepare yourself for the process of changing people, things, practices and your mindset. What are you wanting, now? Who is in your life, now? What are you doing in your life, now? Then, *reevaluate* those things. What behaviors or habits should you break? What people should you remove from your life? What are you doing that is hindering your progress? Write down the week recaps of the different weeks and then you can start the process of purging the unwanted and unnecessary things that are holding you back.

"Don't follow someone who isn't going anywhere or who has never been where you are trying to go."- Cindy Trimm (Previal)

DAY 30

LET GO

After you evaluate and reevaluate, you have to take action to *let go*. In order to live a new life, you must leave an old life; that goes for your negative thoughts as well (breaking negativity). We have discussed many things to let go of in this book, including detrimental people, bad habits, negative mind set and the like. But how often are you letting go? How can you prove that you have let go? Sure, forgiveness is a way to start the process, but how can you be sure that you have committed to this process? A peaceful mind. If you are still finding reasons to avoid someone, something, or someplace because of the stress that it once brought you, you don't have peace of mind. Similar to facing your fears: when someone confronts their fears, they notice that they are still alive and that they have made it through the storm. They realize that is was all in their mind. The same goes for you, at your job, with your boss, and at your school; you have to be able to walk in there, around those people, in those places, like nothing anyone has said, or done, nothing a relationship has wounded, nothing on your mind but peacefulness and excitement for the promise of a wonderful life and future.

This. Will. Be. Difficult. I would be lying if I said I haven't struggled with it. But it takes practice, patience, prayer, and persistence. Cindy Trimm also notes a brilliant illustration about the 360 degree door in her book *"Prevail."* She noted, If you've ever seen one of those circular revolving doors, you know that you have only three options: go around and around in the same (miserable) circular motion, leave out of the same spot you entered, or push forward and exit out on the other side. Healing is important. If you can't change it, there is no use in worrying about it. Don't stay where you are or keep going in circles, push forward to the other side and leave the negativity behind you.

DAY 31

BE ACCOUNATBLE

You can be given all of the tools, you can have done all of the reading, and you could have made great leaps and bounds in this process of breaking negativity, creating positivity, and making it a habit i.e. evaluating, reevaluating, and taking action to *let go*. However, without holding yourself accountable for producing a *daily* desired outcome, you've merely read a book and made no life change. The point isn't to read the book, feel good for a few days, and then go back to living in pain and misery day by day, moment by moment. You are going to have to hold yourself accountable. This is *your* life. I can tell you all of the experiences that I have been through and the stories of others, but the only story that truly matters is yours. Your journey is not something far in the distance. Your journey is in the little moments of everyday, the now. How are you going to fix your moments of anger? How are you going to stay motivated to complete your goals and tasks for the day? How are you going to heal your pain, your circumstances, and your brokenness? What is your plan?

This has been a journey for me as well; I was writing the content of this book in a timely manner of experiencing these situations and this book means more to me than a "first book accomplishment" on the check-list of things to do before I die. This is my heart and soul, this is my healing through helping others (through helping you). I want for you to leave with this in a peaceful way of thinking, a confident way of being, and be assured about the promises of your future. I've made it, and so can you. I am still progressing in my journey and so are you!

God performs miracles, God provides a way when it seems like there is no way. But He only moves with your permission. You have to ask Him to come into your life and help you hold yourself accountable for your promise. Things won't work unless you do.

I was attending World Changers Church International in Atlanta, Georgia and Pastor Creflo Dollar gave a sermon that painted a perfect illustration about the power of authority (and accountability) for my life. He said, "think of Georgia Power, they have given you the electricity (power) for your home, but a light doesn't come on until you flip the switch." He continued, "everything you need has already been made available, all you need to do is flip the switch." It's time for you to flip the switch on your life. You are the only one who can create a better, positive, and more fulfilling life for yourself. It takes effort to "flip the switch" when negativity arises. However, I know you are fully equipped and ready to start implementing life changes!

I'll leave you with this prayer:

Serenity Prayer

God grant me the serenity
to accept the things I cannot change;
courage to change the things I can;
and wisdom to know the difference.
Living one day at a time;
Enjoying one moment at a time;
Accepting hardships as the pathway to peace;
Taking, as He did, this sinful world
as it is, not as I would have it;
Trusting that He will make all things right
if I surrender to His Will;
That I may be reasonably happy in this life
and supremely happy with Him
Forever in the next.
Amen.

--Reinhold Niebuhr

NOTES

NOTES

NOTES

NOTES

NOTES

NOTES

REFERENCES

Amoruso, S. (2015). *#Girlboss*. New York, NY: Portfolio/Penguin and G. P. Putnam's Sons.

Coelho, P., Coelho, P., & Clarke, A. (1993). *The alchemist*. San Francisco: Harper, SanFrancisco.

Deutschman, Alan. *The Second Coming of Steve Jobs*. New York: Broadway, 2000. Print.

Jones-Pothier, K. (2015). *Beautifully broken*. Bloomington, IN: Authorhouse.

Osteen, J. (2015). *You can, you will: 8 undeniable qualities of a winner*. FaithWords.

Soukup, R. (2014). *Living well, spending less: 12 secrets of the good life*. Zondervan.

Thomas, E. (2011). *The secret to success: When you want to succeed as bad as you want to breathe*. Atlanta, GA: Spirit Reign Publishing.

Trimm, C. (2011). *40 day soul fast*. Shippingspurg, PA: Destiny Image Pub.

Foreword T.D. Jakes

Trimm, Cindy, and Paul S. Morton. *Prevail: Discover Your Strength in Hard Places*. Print.

Health Information, Resources, Tools & News Online | Everyday Health. (n.d.). Retrieved March 15, 2016, from http://www.everydayhealth.com/

ABOUT THE AUTHOR

Positive, determined and resilient, Ashley "Colleen" Donald has a creative and ambitious spirit with experience in radio, social media, music entertainment, and vocal performance.

Ashley Donald was born in Saint Petersburg, Florida, August 1st 1990. Her love for music began in her early childhood. Ashley was accepted into the music magnet programs in middle-school and high-school; from 2001-2008 she practiced classical music, took music theory courses, acted in plays and sang in chorus. Ashley really began to take her dreams seriously and began branding herself in college. In 2008, her first year at Saint Petersburg College, Ashley went by the artist and personality name "Ms. Ad." That was her pivotal year, she began connecting with local artist *(Dynasty, Aych, Bluu Zone, Cristol, Trag, Eface, and The Bums etc.)*, singing in talent shows, at graduations and networking within the Tampa/Saint Petersburg music scene; eventually changing her personality and stage name to "Ashli Redd" and cultivating a local name for herself. Continuing to pursue a singing career, she auditioned for American Idol at the age of 18 and made it to the producers round; shortly after, she decided to take a break from music and expand into other areas of entertainment.

Expanding on her love for music and entertainment, she transferred to the University of South Florida as a Media and Culture Communication major and she obtained a creative writing internship at *WTOG CW44 Television*. While working at her internship she also participated and developed two radio shows *"The Redd Paige"* and *"Simply Outrageous"* on *Bulls Radio*). After creating her own websites, blogging, discussing on different media topics and working on different projects, it inspired her to continue work in radio and television.

After graduating with her B.A. in Communication from the University of South Florida in 2012, she began working for *Cox Media Group* radio. Ashley, also known as Ashli Redd during this time, worked in their Promotions Department as a Promotions Assistant as well as a Board Operator in their Programming Department for *Hot101.5, 102.5 The Bone, 97X,* and *Magic 94.9*. While working at *Cox Media Group-Radio* she began developing an idea for an online show, "The Hot Seat." It wasn't reviewed or accepted and after 2 years she decided that it was time for a market change; she took a leap of faith and moved to Atlanta, Georgia.

Since September 2014, she has been building connections and has worked for and volunteered with *A.E.B.L (Atlanta Entertainment Basketball League), Radio One-Hot 107.9, UBA-Georgia Spartans, ICreate LLC,* and has built relationships within *WSB-TV Channel 2, SCB-TV 182* and *92.9 The Game.*

She continues to act and sing when called to the opportunity and has held positions as a part-time Promotions Assistant with the *Atlanta Hawks* basketball team and the *Gwinnett Braves* baseball team. In 2015 she decided to adopt her middle name Colleen instead of her first name (Ashley) to build a fresh start and rebuild

her brand. Colleen is working on developing her own show with *SCB-TV Channel 182*, is a fitness competitor, and is currently in the Master's in Integrated Communication program at Kennesaw State University. She continues to inspire and motivate others throughout her journey.

www.icreateleadership.org

Email: icreateincatl@gmail.com

STAY CONNECTED!

GET HEALTHY!

Follow the Get Healthy Facebook group for inspiration.

www.facebook.com/GHealthy

Facebook:

www.facebook.com/shescolleen

Twitter: shescolleen

Instagram: shescolleen

Inquiries can be emailed to a.colleendonald@gmail.com

Temporary website: www.cargocollective.com/shescolleen
Projected new website: February 2017

www.ingramcontent.com/pod-product-compliance
Lightning Source LLC
LaVergne TN
LVHW041259080426
835510LV00009B/797